VALERIE BODDEN

grow with me

EAGLE

CREATIVE ● EDUCATION

Published by Creative Education
P.O. Box 227, Mankato, Minnesota 56002
Creative Education is an imprint of
The Creative Company
www.thecreativecompany.us

Design by Ellen Huber
Production by Chelsey Luther
Art direction by Rita Marshall
Printed in the United States of America

Photographs by Alamy (Nature Picture Library, Ron
Niebrugge), Dreamstime (Volodymyrkrasyuk), Getty
Images (Jeff Foott, Image by Chris Frank, Peter Lewis,
Klaus Nigge, Keren Su, Roy Toft, Jeremy Woodhouse),
iStockphoto (LoriSkelton), National Geographic (KLAUS
NIGGE, WILD WONDERS OF EUROPE/SHPILENOK/
NATUREPL.COM), Shutterstock (costas anton
dumitrescu, Critterbiz, Inna_77, Eric Isselee, Al Mueller,
Jane Rix), SuperStock (Animals Animals, Biosphoto,
imagebroker.net, Juniors, Steve Bloom Images)

Library of Congress Cataloging-in-Publication Data
Bodden, Valerie.
Eagle / Valerie Bodden.
p. cm. — (Grow with me)
Includes bibliographical references and index.
Summary: An exploration of the life cycle and life span
of eagles, using up-close photographs and step-by-step
text to follow an eagle's growth process from egg to
eaglet to mature eagle.

ISBN 978-1-60818-405-7
1. Eagles—Juvenile literature. 2. Eagles—Life cycles—
Juvenile literature. I. Title.
QL696.F32B625 2014
598.9'42156—dc23   2013029623

CCSS: RI.3.1, 2, 3, 4, 5, 6, 7, 8; RI.4.1, 2, 3, 4, 5, 7; RF.3.3, 4

9 8 7 6 5 4 3 2

TABLE OF CONTENTS

4 *The white-tailed eagle's long talons help it land on ice.*

Eagles are birds known as raptors. They kill and eat other animals such as rabbits, fish, or even monkeys. Eagles have sharp eyesight. This helps them spot **prey** from high in the air. They have strong, hooked beaks and long, curved claws called talons.

There are 59 eagle **species**. Eagles can be found everywhere in the world except in Antarctica. Some eagles survive cold winters on mountains or grasslands. Others like to live in hot deserts or **tropical rainforests**.

5

6

Eagles are some of the world's largest raptors. The biggest eagles can weigh up to 20 pounds (9 kg). Female eagles are usually bigger than males.

To glide, an eagle rides a warm updraft called a thermal.

7

Even though eagles are so big, they are amazing fliers. Their long, wide wings help them **glide** through the air. Some eagles can fly up to 14,000 feet (4,267 m) above the ground!

Eagle eggs are about the size of a tennis ball or a baseball.

Mother eagles lay one to three eggs in a large nest. The eggs are between two and five inches (5–13 cm) long. Eagle eggs can be white, light blue, green, or spotted.

A baby eagle inside an egg is called an **embryo** (*EM-bree-oh*). The embryo gets food from the **yolk** of the egg. The egg has to be kept warm so that the embryo can grow. The mother and father eagle take turns **incubating** the egg. They protect the egg from **predators** such as squirrels, crows, and raccoons.

9

Bald eagles build nests out of sticks near water sources.

10

*Eaglets are also
called "hatchlings"
when they exit
the shell.*

After 30 to 60 days (depending on the species), the egg is ready to hatch. The baby eagle chips at the shell with its egg tooth. This is a hard bump on its beak. It can take up to two days for the baby eagle to get out of its shell!

The newborn eagle is called an eaglet. It is covered with white or gray **down**. The parents take turns bringing food back to the nest for their babies. They rip off small pieces of meat to put in the eaglets' mouths.

11

Bald eagles have the fastest growth rate of North American birds.

Eagle parents keep their talons balled up to avoid hurting young.

12

For the first month or longer, one parent always stays with the eaglets in the nest. The adult keeps the eaglets warm. It also keeps them safe from hawks, bears, and other predators.

Sometimes, the oldest eaglet will hurt its younger brothers or sisters. It might steal the younger eaglets' food. Sometimes the oldest eaglet even kills the younger ones.

Eagles will scare
away birds that fly
too close to the nest.

13

An eaglet's legs turn yellow when it is about three weeks old.

Sea eagles (such as white-tailed eagles) eat a lot of fish.

A baby eaglet grows quickly. It gains one pound (0.5 kg) or more each week. By the time it is three weeks old, the bird is about one foot (30.5 cm) tall.

When it is four or five weeks old, the eaglet learns to rip up its own food. But it is always hungry! The parents leave the eaglet in the nest, and they both go out to hunt.

15

At five or six weeks of age, the eaglet begins to grow flight feathers. The eaglet starts flapping its wings when it is 8 to 10 weeks old. It might even get itself into the air above the nest!

Soon the eaglet makes short flights to the branches around the nest. It practices landing. When it is about 12 weeks old, it makes its first flight!

16

Eaglets stand up in the nest at four to five weeks old.

A harpy eagle is ready to fly in five to six months.

18

Even once an eaglet has learned to fly, its parents still feed it. They will keep feeding it for about six more weeks. Next, the eaglet learns to hunt.

Fish can slip through even the sharp talons of an eagle.

19

The eaglet follows its parents and watches them as they hunt. It also learns by trying to catch prey itself. At first, it does not have much success.

Tawny eagles in Africa often eat carrion or steal food from other birds.

20

An eagle leaves its parents when it is four or five months old. It is now able to take care of itself. The eagle sits on a branch or soars through the air, watching for prey. When the young eagle spots prey, it dives through the air to grab it. If the eagle finds **carrion**, it will eat that, too.

Fully grown eagles have no natural predators. But people sometimes hurt eagles. They cut down trees and pollute eagles' homes. Many eagle species are now **endangered**.

Bald eagles were removed from the endangered species list in 2007.

21

Eagles in Europe may migrate, but many are hardy enough to survive colder temperatures.

Some eagles **migrate** each year in search of food. In the fall, they fly south. They return north in the spring. Eagles that eat fish need to find places where the water does not freeze.

Young eagles often migrate earlier in the fall than adults. They stay in their winter home longer than older eagles. Migrating eagles fly alone but sometimes gather in large groups.

23

Eagles group together only when food is to be found.

Eagles **molt** every year. A young eagle's new feathers are different colors than the ones it lost. When the eagle is four or five years old, it gets its adult coloring.

The eagle is now fully grown. It looks for a mate by doing flying tricks called flight displays. Eagles mate for life.

Eagles with locked talons spin through the air before parting.

Preening is the process of cleaning and straightening feathers.

25

26

Disk-shaped nests
are built on level
places such as
rock ledges.

A male that wants to mate will bring twigs to a female's nest.

Eagle mates work together to build a large nest called an aerie (*AIR-ee*). Aeries are usually built on top of tall trees or high cliffs. The birds add on to the nest each year. Some nests are more than six feet (1.8 m) wide and deep!

Five to 10 days after mating, the female lays an egg in the nest. A day or two later, she usually lays another egg. One more egg may follow a day or two after that.

Most eagles live 15 to 30 years. If an eagle's mate dies, the eagle may take a new mate. Someday, that eagle will die, too. But its young will live on. They will lay eggs of their own. And new eagles will be born.

An eaglet counts on its parents to give it food and help it grow.

Some eagles lay
several clutches,
or groups of eggs,
per year.

29

A female eagle lays her  eggs in a nest.

An embryo begins growing in each egg.

 After 30 to 60 days, the eaglet hatches.

One parent stays with the eaglet  for the first 4 or 5 weeks.

The eaglet begins to grow flight feathers at 5 or 6 weeks.

At 12 weeks old, the eaglet makes its first flight.

When it is 4 or 5 months old, the eaglet leaves its parents.

An eagle looks for a mate at 4 or 5 years old.

After 15 to 30 years, the eagle dies.

carrion: *the rotting flesh of dead animals*

down: *soft, fluffy feathers that cover a baby bird when it is first born*

embryo: *an offspring that has not hatched out of an egg yet*

endangered: *in danger of dying out, so that no more of that animal are left in the world*

glide: *to move through the air without flapping wings*

incubating: *sitting on eggs to keep them warm as the embryo inside grows*

migrate: *to move from place to place during different parts of the year, usually to find food and warmth*

molt: *to lose old feathers and grow new ones*

predators: *animals that kill and eat other animals*

prey: *animals that are killed and eaten by other animals*

species: *groups of living things that are closely related*

tropical rainforests: *hot and wet places where many plants grow; they are found in the hottest parts of the world*

yolk: *the middle, yellow part of an egg that contains food for a growing embryo*

WEBSITES

National Geographic Kids: Bald Eagle Facts and Pictures

http://kids.nationalgeographic.com/kids/animals/creaturefeature/baldeagle/

Check out facts, pictures, and videos of bald eagles.

The Peregrine Fund: Eagles

http://www.peregrinefund.org/subsites/explore-raptors-2001/eagles/eaglmain.html

Learn more about the different kinds of eagles.

Note: Every effort has been made to ensure that the websites listed above are suitable for children, that they have educational value, and that they contain no inappropriate material. However, because of the nature of the Internet, it is impossible to guarantee that these sites will remain active indefinitely or that their contents will not be altered.

READ MORE

Morgan, Sally. *Eagles.*
Mankato, Minn.: Amicus, 2011.

Riggs, Kate. *Eagles.*
Mankato, Minn.: Creative Education, 2012.

INDEX